How We Use Maps

by Kelly Gaffney

Look at all the maps.

This is a very big map.

And this is a little map.

It can fit in your hand!

You can see a lake on this map.

The lake on the map is blue.

You can see roads on this map.

The roads on the map are white.

Look at the school.

It is a very big school.

Here is a map of a school.

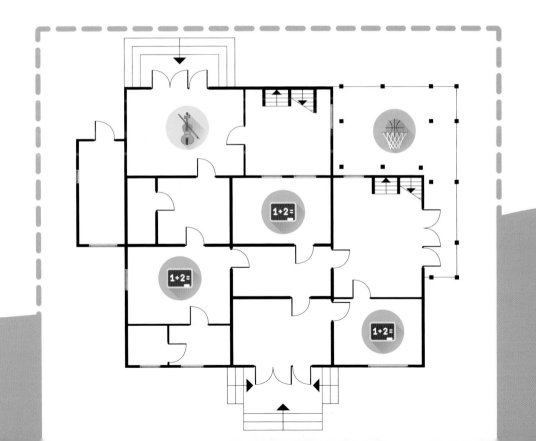

This map can help you get to the zoo.

This is a map of the zoo.

It can help you look

for the animals.

This is a map of the shops.

The map can help you
get to the bike shop.

This is my house.

I have a map of my house.

I have a map of my room!

Can you see my bed?

Can you see me?

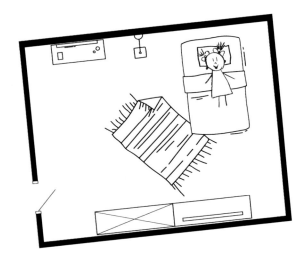